ORDINARY
PEOPLE
CHANGE
— THE —
WORLD

I am Frida Kahlo

BRAD MELTZER

illustrated by Christopher Eliopoulos

ROCKY POND BOOKS

I am FRIDA KAHLO.

I was born in Mexico in this house. Later, we painted it blue and called it La Casa Azul—the Blue House.
It stood out from everything else.
Isn't that beautiful?

When I was six years old, I got a disease called polio.
It made my right leg thinner and shorter than my left leg.

I had to stay in my room for nine months.
When I finally got out, kids would make fun of me.

I tried hiding my leg under long skirts or by wearing extra socks.
It didn't help.

Thankfully, I always had a special place where I could escape. In my room, I'd breathe onto the windowpane and draw a door.

That door let me enter my imagination.

There, I would visit a dairy called Pinzón.
I entered through the O.

It would take me
down, down, down
inside the earth . . .

where my imaginary friend was always waiting for me.

I don't remember what she looked like, or even what color she was.

But together, we would laugh and dance.

I'd tell her all my problems—and she would listen.

That place made me happy.
And when I'd blur the door with my hand, it would disappear.

It's amazing what you can do with your imagination.

To strengthen my leg, my dad encouraged me to play sports:
Soccer, wrestling, boxing, swimming, I did it all.

One of the best things my dad shared with me was his curiosity about the world. As a photographer, he'd take me along when he went to shoot photos.

OKAY, PLANTS, SAY CHEESE!

He also liked to paint.
While he did his watercolors, I'd collect pebbles, plants, and even insects.

I'd bring them home, looking up each item in my dad's books and examining them under a microscope.

Look around. Beauty is everywhere.

At fourteen, I went to the National Preparatory School, the best high school in Mexico.

Of the two thousand students, I was one of only thirty-five girls.

At school, we were supposed to dress and behave a certain way.
I dressed . . . differently.
The wealthy mothers would take one look at me and yell . . .

To other students, I was fascinating.

My closest friends were a group of kids called the Cachuchas, which is like a hot pepper.

We were smart and loved to read. But sometimes we got in trouble, like when we rode a real donkey down the hallway!

One day, a famous painter named Diego Rivera was hired to create a mural in our auditorium. I watched him for three hours.

I didn't know it at the time, but my hardest days were coming.

At eighteen, I was in a terrible accident, when a trolley smashed into the bus I was riding.

Someone on the bus had been carrying paint, so my body was covered in powdered gold.

A month after the accident, I came home from the hospital in a full body cast.

My spinal column was broken in three places.

The doctors literally had to put me back together.

The pain in my leg and foot was terrible, and I could barely move my arms.

But I survived.

I didn't get many visitors.

It made me realize that I wanted to be friends only with people who like me just the way I am.

Since I couldn't sit up in bed, my mom asked a carpenter
to make a special easel for me.
I grabbed my father's brushes.
Then I began.

I worked hard, poring over books about art history.

My first paintings weren't great.
I even tore one up because I was so unhappy with it.
But with my mirror, I kept going, painting what I saw.

I paint myself because I am so often alone
and because I am the subject I know best.

As soon as I could go outside, I brought my paintings to Diego Rivera, the famous painter I had met years earlier.

Over time, my portraits became more complex.
I began adding pieces of local Mexican art and history—
textiles and intricate carvings—to show people who I was.

Eventually, Diego and I got married.
We traveled to America, to places like San Francisco, New York, and Detroit, meeting some of the wealthiest people in the world.

Just like in high school, some people would insult my clothing.

My time away made me realize that my favorite place of all . . .

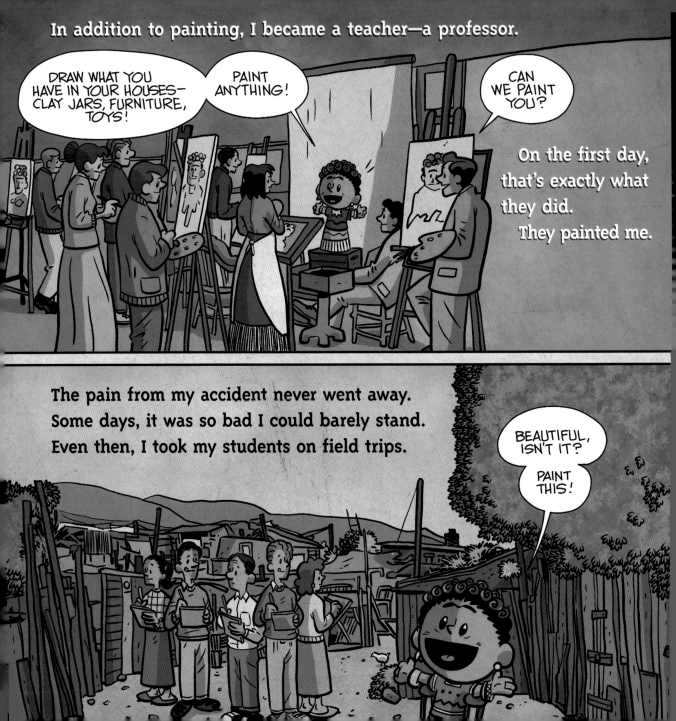

As my health got worse, my four most committed students—
Los Fridos—came to my Casa Azul for their lessons.

Eventually, I sent them out into the world, to paint murals on
nearby laundries and taverns.

To honor my work, a gallery owner began planning my first-ever one-woman show in Mexico.

PHOTOGRAPHER LOLA ALVAREZ BRAVO

I was so sick, she was worried I might miss it.
So they set up my bed and made me part of the exhibit.

It was total chaos.
And absolutely beautiful.

Tragedy nearly took my life.
But it couldn't take my spirit.
Fighting back wasn't easy,
especially when people made fun of how I looked
and where I was from.
But I was determined to see things
differently.

My face, my clothes, my country, even my pain—
these are the colors on my canvas.
They don't look like anyone else's,
and they shouldn't.
That's the best part.
Your picture is uniquely yours.

Art is like life.
It's rarely what it first appears.
Instead of following a straight path,
your life and your art will twist and turn,
taking you on unexpected journeys.

It's messy and bold and scary and fun.
But it's all part of your picture—a magnificent self-portrait.

I am Frida Kahlo,
and I know that the
most beautiful thing is
you—just as you are.

"Painting completed my life."
—FRIDA KAHLO

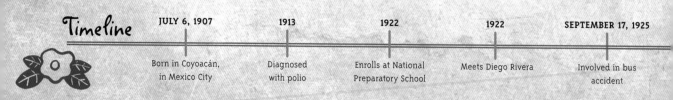

Timeline

JULY 6, 1907	1913	1922	1922	SEPTEMBER 17, 1925
Born in Coyoacán, in Mexico City	Diagnosed with polio	Enrolls at National Preparatory School	Meets Diego Rivera	Involved in bus accident

....
Frida at age 11

....
Frida with Diego Rivera

....
Frida (third from left)
with her sisters
and cousins

1929	1943	1953	JULY 13, 1954	1958
Marries Diego Rivera	Begins as professor at La Esmeralda School	Solo exhibition in Mexico	Dies in Coyoacán	Frida Kahlo Museum opens

For Pansy and Rob Price,
who thankfully,
with artist souls,
never do anything like anyone else
–B.M.

For Javier Villegas, Hilda,
Humberto, and the rest of the
folks at La Cava del Tequila for
always making me feel at home
–C.E.

For historical accuracy, we used Frida Kahlo's actual words whenever possible. For more of
her true voice, we recommend and acknowledge the below works.

··

SOURCES

Frida: A Biography of Frida Kahlo by Hayden Herrera (Harper, 2002)

Frida by Frida by Raquel Tibol (Editorial RM, Mexico, 2003)

You are Always With Me. Letters to Mama 1923–1932 by Frida Kahlo. Edited and translated by Héctor Jaimes (Virago Press, UK, 2018)

Frida Kahlo: Making Her Self Up Edited by Claire Wilcox & Circe Henestrosa

Frida Kahlo at Home by Suzanne Barbezat

FridaKahlo.org

MuseoFridaKahlo.org

FURTHER READING FOR KIDS

Frida Kahlo and Her Animalitos by Monica Brown and John Parra (NorthSouth Books, 2017)

Who Was Frida Kahlo? by Sarah Fabiny (Penguin Workshop, 2013)

Viva Frida by Yuyi Morales (Roaring Brook Press, 2014)

Women Artists A to Z by Melanie LaBarge and Caroline Corrigan (Dial, 2020)

WHERE TO SEE FRIDA KAHLO'S PAINTINGS

Frida Kahlo Museum, Mexico City, Mexico

Museo de Arte Moderno, Mexico City, Mexico

Museum of Modern Art, New York City

National Museum of Women in the Arts, Washington, DC

···

ROCKY POND BOOKS • An imprint of Penguin Random House LLC, New York

First published in the United States of America by Dial Books for Young Readers, an imprint of Penguin Random House LLC, 2021.
This edition published by Rocky Pond Books, an imprint of Penguin Random House LLC, 2023. • Text copyright © 2021 by Forty-four Steps, Inc. • Illustrations copyright © 2021 by Christopher Eliopoulos

Rocky Pond Books and colophon are trademarks of Penguin Random House LLC. • The Penguin colophon is a registered trademark of Penguin Books Limited.

Visit us online at penguinrandomhouse.com.

Library of Congress Cataloging-in-Publication Data is available.

Reproductions of Frida Kahlo's artwork © Banco de México Diego Rivera Frida Kahlo Museums Trust, Mexico, D.F. / Artists Rights Society (ARS), New York.
With thanks as well to the Frida Kahlo Corporation. All photos of Frida Kahlo (pages 38–39) by Guillermo Kahlo; Public Domain.

ISBN 9780525555988 • Manufactured in China • 10 9 8 7
TOPL
Designed by Jason Henry • Text set in Triplex • The artwork for this book was created digitally.

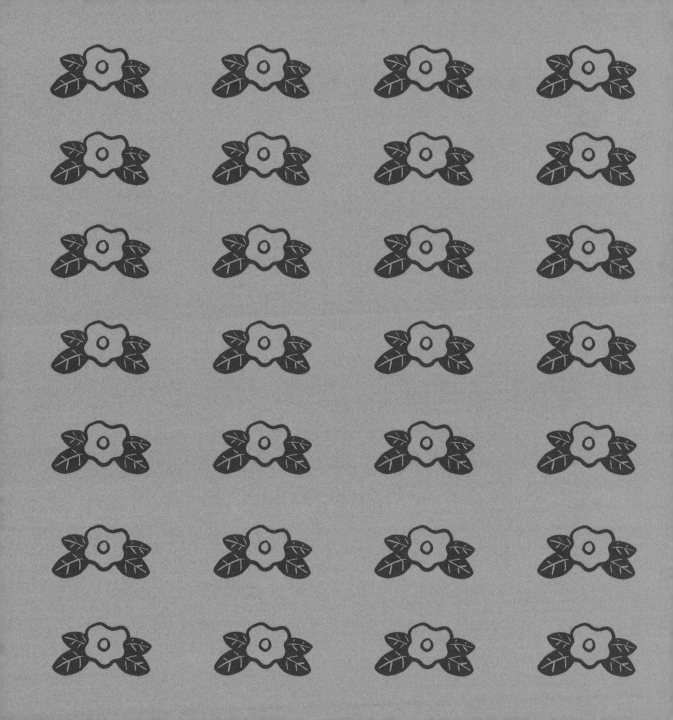